MOON SPIRIT
Love Poems of A Mated Woman

for Richard

my beloved husband,
who nourishes and appreciates
the fullest flowering of
my womanhood

and for my parents

Father, now a bright star
of the night sky
and
Mother,
a beautiful flower
who blooms among us still

MOON SPIRIT
Love Poems of A Mated Woman

Poems, Photographs and Sketches

by Eleanore Kosydar

TP

TIERCERON PRESS

Copyright © 1998 by Eleanore Kosydar

Published by: **TIERCERON PRESS**
76 Maple Ave.
Dundas, ON Canada L9H 4W4
Tel. (905) 628-9092

Canadian Cataloguing in Publication Data

Kosydar, Eleanore, 1941-
    Moon spirit : love poems of a mated woman :
poems, photographs and sketches

ISBN 0-9694077-2-6

    I. Title.

PS8571.08845M66 1997   C811'.54   C97-901245-7
PR9199.3.K68M66 1997

Typeface is *Original Garamond*

Printed and bound in Canada by Friesens

ACKNOWLEDGMENTS

The drawing on page 49 was created especially for this book by my friend, artist Pamela Sinclair. Thank you, Pam—you have evoked the magic of childhood with this beautiful and sensitive portrayal of your young son.

Writing the poems in this collection has been a moving and often profound experience, expanding my awareness and appreciation of the many dimensions of love.

I feel blessed to have been born into a loving family, where I believe a capacity for happiness and contentment is learned. For this I am eternally grateful to my parents.

To each of my siblings, I give fond and heartfelt thanks: Mary, travelling companion of my youth—for encouragement, support and helpful suggestions regarding my poems, and for your amazing haiku to Richard and me (page 33); Liisa, my childhood pal—for your gentle, thoughtful listening to an early draft of this book, and cherished response, and for the lovely gift of wind chimes which inspired *"Silver and Gold"* (page 26); and Dave, for your enthusiastic response to the poems and for being a warm soul with a certain attachment to a pole.

I wish to express grateful appreciation to members of the Tower Poetry Society, and to my gifted creative writing group (Paula, Joanna and Sheila), and my dear friend Mary and the other bright lights of our bi-weekly Salon: Thank you, all—for inspiration, stimulating discussions, and valuable feedback in the development of my poetry. Special thanks to Janelle, for lending your keen eye and mind to a review of the final draft; and to Denise, for sowing a seed.

How do I adequately thank the mate with whom my life is intimately woven? My husband, Richard provided valuable technical and other assistance in the production of this book, and contributed an elegant photograph of a mute swan, all of which are much appreciated. More important, to him is due the underlying essence and very existence of this poetry, which speaks for itself.

Previously published poems included in this collection are:

The Touch of Love (*1995 Top 40 Anthology of Hamilton Area Poets*)
Tower of Love (*Tower Poetry*, Winter 1995-96, Vol. 44 No. 2)
To Elizabeth Barrett Browning (*Canadian Author*, June 97)

CONTENTS

The Greeting, 11

Kissed by Love, 12

This Gift, 13

Love for a Golden Age, 14

Moon Spirit, 17

The Touch of Love, 18

Your Hands, 19

The Kiss, 20

Summer Love, 21

At the Waterfall of Poets, 22

Movements of the Heart, 24

My Song to the Moon, 25

Silver & Gold, 26

Mated, 26

Fated, 27

Man & Woman, 28

Love Garden I, 30

To Elizabeth Barrett Browning, 32

From A Sage Sister, by Mary Hendrix, 33

To the Sage Sister, 33

Love's Pain, 34

Tower of Love, 36

As the River Loves the Sea, 37

Portrait of My Mother, 39

Water and Rock, 43

For My Father: I. Father, Star, 44
II. Star Gazer, 45

Bless the Child, 48

Song to the Earth, 50

Our Lap Luxurious, 52

Love is a River, 53

Ode to Love, 54

Love Garden II, 56

To My Husband
Nearing Our Silver Anniversary, 58

Love Made with Love, 60

Tender Nights of Love, 61

Tiger Nights, 62

Ordinary Things, 63

Ecstasy, 64

Reflections of Love, 66

Meditation on 'Namaste,' 67

Quiet Joy, 68

Our Love Is A Sacred Thing! 69

Feted, 70

Prayer of Thanks, 71

THE GREETING

Namaste![*]
May love bless your way!
The good and peace in me
greet the good and
peace in thee.

[*]Nam'–as–té is a traditional Hindu greeting used upon meeting or parting,
given with hands held vertically, palms facing, in front of the bosom.

KISSED BY LOVE

A wanderer through life was I,
A wanderer were you:
Travelling the road of life
   But always passing through.

Then fortune smiled upon my way
And drew me near to you:
Your path crossed mine
   or mine crossed yours—
And we began anew.

Our pathways intersected
Along life's dusty road;
Our lives interconnected—
   Love kissed a place we strode.

Awandering we'll go no more
For we've been kissed, my dear!
Kissed by blessed Love we were
   And now the road shines clear.

Forever more we'll find our way
Along sweet haven's shore;
Abode of Love's eternal kiss,
   Wanderers no more.

THIS GIFT

To love and be loved~
For this gift eternal thanks
to Heaven above

LOVE FOR A GOLDEN AGE

Human hearts yearn for a Golden Age
   long for love
   wish for beauty, hope for truth;
   wistfully picture a life of perfect luxury,
                        wealth, ease...

Seekers of life's gold
mistaking what gold is
   imagine it to lie without
   pursue it as objects to behold
   seek coins, fabric, jewels, art
        find such gold cold and without heart;

The seeker within
will learn what gold truly is:
   discover its mystery
   uncover its history
   learn its complexity
   and gain in the search
        unimagined riches; gifts of golden spirit.

The human heart hungers for love
but mistaking what love is
   pursues passion
   is misled by fashion
   is from objects of desire soon parted
        often disappointed and downhearted;

The seeker within
will discover what love is:
   will find it is trust, not lust
   will strive to understand, not demand
   will pursue the good not of one, but two
        faithfully;   with patience
           and respect, hand in hand;

will learn to give   and to forgive,
       in giving finding love that endures
and grow to know that the brightest gold shines
          from the hold of a loving heart.

Free of guile, any heart can love
and loving, find living gold of rare compare.
       Life being life   and humans human,
       all cannot be golden, nor love always rare
            nor will all the loved return love fair;

       Yet love's gold lies within the reach
       of each giving heart that seeks:
            Finding love, found only within,
            any age can be golden
               illumined by love's luminescent glow.

     Going forth, giving freely of
       the gift of our own golden love
          we each partake in the exquisite grace
              of our own   Golden Age!

MOON SPIRIT

I, woman   am kin to the moon
heavenly body of phases and cycles
mountained and cratered
tempering Sol's blaze

Circles   within circles
circle;   Luna,
Heavenly Body of Lovers
silvery, soft-edged
mysterious
shimmers,   tantalizing
with her hints
of the partly known;
changes,   inviting
discovery
revealing secrets
of the lover soul

Luminous orb
of lustrous light
pours silver
stillness
over the world
Imagination soars
in moonlight
Love blooms
dazzled, crazed
in moonlight

I, woman
wedded to sun
and kin to the moon
soft-edged, mysterious
bare for you   in moonlight
                    my lover soul

THE TOUCH OF LOVE

The touch of love

    brushes soft as a dove
    blushing lips with crimson stains;

    cleaves close as a glove
    clasping firm its golden grains;

    reaches deep from skies above
    rippling stars through burnished veins;

    shivers rhapsodies of whispered love
    coursing sweet with hearts' refrains—

        and speaks silent volumes thereof.

YOUR HANDS

From when we first met
I have loved your hands.

They speak to me straight
from your heart
speak   of strength
and of gentleness and love
of beauty and art.

I am touched
by their aesthetic form:
manly, well-proportioned hands
not over-large; broader than mine
(which tuck into them neat
and snug) and slightly longer.

I marvel at their
deftness; am moved
by their crafting of gesture:
sensitive hands   holding and
cradling all you handle
with caring respect;
materials   as I, responsive
to their touch.

They radiate warmth from your
inner core, seem reservoirs
of the very breath
of life—express
the essence of you, reveal
why   from the first
I   now your wife
have loved your hands.

The Kiss

Fervent bliss of ardent lovers
Simple movement, but profound
Starts within, the silent stirring
Heart's aflutter, on the wing
Affection, passion want expression
Seek release from quivering

My lips are stirred but not to speak
Their message they impress upon you
Tell of welling deep emotion
Press, caress you, trembling
Taste of mystic purple potion
Drink, Dear Love! Our full lips sing!

SUMMER LOVE

A Book of Verses underneath the Bough
A Jug of Wine, a Loaf of Bread—and Thou
Beside me singing in the Wilderness—
Oh, Wilderness were Paradise enow!

from ***Rubaiyat of Omar Khayyam***
(transl. by Edward Fitzgerald)

Here we lie beneath a Bough
    of greenest green
    Flower Perfume wafts on silken Air
    Summer Breezes ripple through our Hair

With Poetry glad Earth endows
    this tranquil Scene
    We drink the Spirit of her sacred Verse,
    Our spirits fed as if Bread were disbursed

Your Head upon my Lap, we vow
    our Love, unseen
    Wild Grasses bow, discreetly swaying
    While Birds twitter Psalms, sweetly praying

My Touch is light upon your Brow,
    I feel your Sheen
    As We linger here in Paradise
    Our Heavenly Earthly Paradise...

AT THE WATERFALL OF POETS

The waterfall sings,
   "I find my song,
      when I find my freedom."

My Love led me to a waterfall,
a waterfall of poets—
   where a sylvan streamlet muses,
   plays sparkling watery music
   on rock; where musing, it calls
   with sweet songs of love.

The place had grown wild,
smothered with tangles
      and careless leavings
   concealing its beauty
   constraining its verse,
   muffling the dear water's call.

With love we cleared the small waterfall
of heedless clutter—bared the rock
   leaving streamwater free to
   tumble and muse and splash and spill
   from ledge to rocky ledge; freely it
   spills from pool to low-lipped pool.

Water cool at the Waterfall of Poets
freed from needless constraint
   cascades silver melodies pure
   and clear. Wetted ardour
   flows free   wild   joyous!
   With love it splashes and pools.

My Love is like that waterfall:
   He's a man whose music
   is temptingly tiered,
   mellifluous, dear; tumbling
   and spilling from pool to pool
   splashing with joyful abandon.

I am like that rock:
   A woman caressed as by water's
   wet ardour—caressed and immersed
   quenching my thirst
   played on and thrilled and
   made to lilt my sweet song of love.

Now we dream lyric dreams at our waterfall,
our Waterfall of Poets
   free-falling, cascading
   sparkling, and pure—
   where Free Spirits three
   sing of love.

MOVEMENTS OF THE HEART

You move
and your movement catches my heart
In a glance   my eyes take you in:
    I notice your face, your slight-smiling face
    your gentle contented in-revealed face
        and my heart is filled with love.

My heart beholds yours:
    true, warm   and kind
    Your deep heart fills my mind
        and my thoughts bathe you in love.

Your movement fills my eyes:
    your cat-like containment
    your poise,   your grace
    your manly body and masculine pace
        and my full self swells with love.

Brimming over
with love
I move
    press my body to yours
    touch my lips to your smile
    brush my cheek across your face,
        place my head on your broad shoulder.
Intertwined
    we abide for a time
    in perfect embrace
        and I purr,   like a cat   content.

MY SONG TO THE MOON

Silvery Luna
bold shimmer
against a backdrop of stars:
Your lovely silken light
fills me with dreams

Shimmering Luna,
I would tempt my lover
with silky promises
and star-studded hope
rouse him to heights
of human desire

Silky Luna,
envelop me in creamy light:
ethereal curves thinly veiled
behind pale clouds
of sheer delight

Dissolving
I'll surrender
singing praises
of your blessed fire:

Lovely Luna,
sacred is your silver fire!

SILVER & GOLD

Ringing silver chimes
circle bands of crafted gold~
Precious vows are told!

MATED

Our souls, man and wife
through struggles, joy, growth and change
are mated for life

FATED

Mated in this life
Fated husband and wife
We dwell on our joy

MAN & WOMAN
This Vision I See

Man & Woman, who are you?
  Do you know just who you are?
    What are your Natures, and your Race?
      Where are the Hallowed Halls you grace?

I, a Woman and you, a Man
  Love as One, yet we are Two.
  Humans both, we differ in View:

  Crests align with Counterpoint;
  with differing oils we each anoint.
  You are Bold where I feel Shy
  yet I will tread where you fear to try.

  I'm more Soft and you're more Firm
  but strength is in me and gentleness in you.
  Tender emotions at my surface lie;
  they burrow in you while tougher ones fly.

  Your talk is pointed, mine soft-edged;
  Misperceptions can get wedged,
  Confusion may rain about our heads…
  But to understanding we're both pledged.

Our Two Perspectives are required
  Tempered, each by its Opposite.
    Both have assets much desired:
      Conjoined they form a Composite.

Man without Woman, how fare you?
   "Sad and lonely; what to do!"
Woman sans Man, where are you?
   Afloat, unmoored; drifting...
                              toward *You*.

Incomplete without the other
   Man wants Woman, and Woman, Man.
      Each a Compass to other's Soul
         We're both needed to make life whole.

This Vision Bright is what I see:
   Together we live on Earth's vibrant shore.
      Our Hands reach out across the Sea~
         In Love & Peace let us each adore.

LOVE GARDEN I

Love &
     Garden
         so   alike
             each in its way
                 links earth & spirit
                     correspondences resonate

Love like a garden grows   luxuriant
  resplendent   many-hued   and richly green
  when lovers sow,   then mutually nurture:
  tend, cultivate, fences mend; keep weeds cleared clean.

Welcome, Love ~ come be my precious garden:
  let me lavish on you all the best of care;
  plunge deep my hands into your fertile soil,
  prepare soft ground   my lover to join me there.

Come, my love, to the garden of shared delight!
  We'll grow gorgeous flowers in amorous air~
  Warm sun will bathe our garden in golden light;
  Gentle rains will sleek her greenly shining hair.

Through dusky nights and sky-blue days we'll tend her
  that coral,   ruby,   gold   might multiply.
  Through drought or thundering storm we'll defend her
  from wither, wilt or bolt   that she'll not die.

> *Garden is earth   cultivated*
> *for fruitfulness, for beauty;*
> *earth   exceptional*
> *in fertility and delight*
> *Is not cultivation an act*
> *of love? and Garden embodiment*
> *of Love? Or symbol...*

Faithfully we've nurtured love, remaining true~
  gratefully reaped profusion of fruit she grows.
Our love still shimmers   new   as morning dew
  but blooms now with the flush of a full-blown rose.

TO ELIZABETH BARRETT BROWNING

How do I thank thee? How best sing thy praise?
Thy tender words which speak of love felt deep
sent passions real with heartfelt truth to leap
from heart to page and page to heart—always
their impact undiminished, kept ablaze
in timeless phrases perfect poems keep.
I've pondered ways my praises high to heap
on wondrous words of love which still amaze
long past thy mortal days. It dawns on me
that I might rightly honour thee with ease
in thine own way! With grateful heart to see
past grave, I pray thy deathless spirit please,
great poetess, accept homage from me
in this, my sonnet   to *"The Portuguese."*

FROM A SAGE SISTER

Sister like petals
Brother-in-law more like thorns
Together, a rose

By Mary Hendrix

TO THE SAGE SISTER

Sister a gentle soul
Brother-in-law gentle, too~
Beauty, truth and love!

LOVE'S PAIN

How is it, Gentle Love, that you hurt so?
   How is it that you cause such grievous pain?
Your hurts are many—too many to name;
   Yet name a few I will, to sad acclaim:

Unrequited love is one,
that awful lover's bane—
passion felt but not returned;
love grown, it seems, in vain

        Love shared then lost leaves
        lingering sadness in its wake
        Clutched too tight it might
        suffocate; or neglected, dissipate;
        or lovers follow differing paths
        until their pairing breaks

Mate sought but never found leaves
a   void
as with children much desired
when nature yields up naught
Emptiness may long persist
in spite of aught...

        Couples, friends have highs and lows
        know times of hurt and anger
        Intentions, words misunderstood?
        Bruised feelings are a danger
        Disagreements volatile
        may escalate, turn hostile
        To the agonies of love
        pairs are not strangers

The wounds unfaithful lovers inflict
strike   to the core—
the betrayed,   dismayed   falter
trust and respect turn tenderly sore

For all who love, distress is deep
when seeing loved ones suffer
during illness, grief or despair
or other severe stress

Death of a beloved is anguish;
a part of self departs when loved ones go
Long days of lonely loss and ache pass slow
ere gratitude for Love surpasses sorrow...

Oh, Gentle Love, I've known some of this pain
   and doubt not that I'll meet with more again.
But I'll not banish you to ease the strain;
   for loveless life would be quite inhumane.

Imagine the soulless existence! Life
   with no love would be comfortless,   abyss.
And the joy, Dear Love! What of your laughter
   and your joy? I will not relinquish this

regardless of the cost. Instead   I choose
   to dwell not on your pain but on your gain:
that wellspring of grace where humankind thrives,
   wherein we find deep meaning for our lives.

I pledge, therefore what I intend to do—
   Mark clearly, with resolve   my life's direction:
With faithful heart, unswervingly   I'll strive
   to amplify my love   until I die.

TOWER OF LOVE

LOVE
rooted deep
and firm
builds
upon
its own
foundations
a lofty
structure
of amazing
creation!
Nourishing
nectar
streams
through
sheltering
bower
Lover and loved
are
drenched
in delectable dews:
Watch them, they *flower*!
Rare beauty blossoms
round that heady
tower
bears fruitful
witness
to
the power
of
LOVE!

As the River Loves the Sea

I kiss you as the bee kisses a flower
and hold you to my breast
    as though an earth embraced her tree.

I smile as summer sun beams from blue skies
and caress you like the breeze
    that whispers lightly with my sighs.

I love you as the river loves the sea...

Come, my love, to me
    like the ruby-throated hummingbird
sip softly petalled nectar by my thigh.

As the rainbowed arch
    gloriously adores her shower,
I will love you like a land embraced by sky.

PORTRAIT OF MY MOTHER
December 1996

Pretty young woman   beside
the brightly lit tree: sweetly you smile
from the burnished frame. A lively
twinkle lights your blue eyes.

Your heart was won by he who loves
to be with you: who sent a note
of high regard, good wishes   and
some four-leaf clovers for good luck!
Wed to him for over half a century,
you wedded yourself   equally   to
your jointly created family and home.
Wholeheartedly devoted to this
domestic trinity,   your life's work
has been work of the heart and hearth.

Heart of the family, heart of the home—
with constant heart you've tended house,
garden, souls; mindful of the needs of each
allowing us each to flower naturally
as individual: wild strawberry, willowy
harebell, vivacious buttercup. Your precious
garden imbued my childhood with magic!
marigolds deepest rust, yellow, ruby;   and
bleeding heart and *lily of the valley*, touches
of soft pink and fairy white (they grow
in my garden still   and always will).

. . . .

Like steadfast Hestia, ancient goddess of
the hearth   you move serenely in your realm
content in homely tasks and responsibilities
sowing, sewing,   lovingly weaving
and crafting   ♥   a calm island
in this frantic world: serving
with simple graciousness foods you make
by hand   baking,   breaking bread
always the home fires warmly burning.
Accepting, non-judgmental, welcoming
all who enter your welcome haven   you
listen to, respect   other's views and
choices,   resist only   what you perceive
to be dangerous or unhealthy.

Sweet-natured, even-tempered, totally fair:
Much   has been asked of your tender heart
in loved ones' struggles with heartache, anger,
adversity.   Loyal helpmate, mother, daughter:
cheerfully you've nursed generations of family
through bouts of illness.   You counter
with compassion the outragious; hearten
our dismay with kindness and hope.

Unable to share your own suffering, you
bear your private pain with the same steady
patience and grace you bring to your love;
constantly do your best, come what may.
Near one eye,   recurrent nerve pain
suggests the strain of troubles you've seen

yet   your warm laughter comes easily, your
ageless smiling face   (never camouflaged)
retains a youthful softness and rosy glow.
And your dear heart only grows
be it joy or sorrow that comes your way...

More reserved than my effusive father
your colour is   *blue* serene and   peaceful
your nature pastel and navy, Scandinavian,
ultramarine   and soft blue-grey   echoing
beloved Superior's rocky shore (we planted
lush *lobelia* there — azure, deep).

Gatherer of pretty stones   ever since
an auspicious roadside find,   your delight
in colours, patterns, texture, form
revealed for me the intrinsic beauty of rock
and the power   of water's shaping role.
I hold in my palm a treasured gift from you
miniature mountain   swirling white at its peak
lusciously red-veined,   heart-like near the base
a favourite agate   brought home long ago
from the "Big Water"   polished with
a jumble of others   in the tumbler Dad built.
Feeling the soft   cool   smoothness of
burnt sienna, white   and grey I walk again
with you   combing the beach, see again
your gentle face   like a tranquil
brush of waves   washing
the rugged shore ...

. . . .

A few months past,   you showed me
the picture of your heart, Mother
the one the doctors took   and it looked
just as I knew it would:
　　　sturdy and sheltering, like an oak
　　　　　strong-branched   a river of love
　　　　　　　lovely violet of perpetual bloom.
Look again, Mother at the picture:
Can you see us there?   your loved ones
twinkling   *forget-me-nots*   woven
inextricably   into the fabric of
your warm, beautiful heart...

Christmas now is here, symbolic anew
of love hope joy.   Upon your tree each year
you place   a small angel   smiling dreamily.
Truly, the angel is *you*   forever framed
in the spirit of the season's light—

*Heart & Hearth merge in you into
a single perfect rhythm   of love's eternal beat:*

With quiet dignity   you wear your heart
on your sleeve,   Mother   and in your eyes
and smile   ♥   Gentle shaper of souls,
your special gifts   are   a beautiful blend
of pink, blue and white: *bountiful
bleeding heart* and   lovely *lobelia*,
with we   *lilies of the valley*
growing   gratefully
at your feet

WATER AND ROCK
(Dedicated to My Mother)

Soft water on hard rock
In your caress of ages
Irresistible strength

For My Father

★ ★ ★ ☆

For we are the stars. For we sing.
For we sing with our light...

       (from a Pasamaquoddy Indian poem)

I. FATHER, STAR

Father, you are ★ a *STAR*
sparkling torch of the infinitude
for you sing with your light

We hear your shining
voice and hearing, see
that star-like we, too might be
beacons along a way
birds of fire
spreading our wings
over the sky

Let us be, then, our star selves
our flaming bird souls

Let us sing with light
voices mingling with yours
and make the heavens   bright
with our fire of joy!

II. STAR GAZER

As a young man
you built a telescope
to study the stars
You tracked the planets
Venus, Jupiter and Mars
...and ever the stars shine on...

The early photograph of you
stays a moment in time:
Blond, blue-eyed lad of nine
poised, dignified
asked to be a man
before your time
your father   gone
from your native Finland
to seek fortune in America
Years later he will come back
bring mother, young brother
and   you   to
this land of promise

In the New World
you work for the good of all
help parents, brothers;
work mostly for others;
your dreams
not of fame or fortune,
    but   family and home
and something indefinable
for the soul:
    for yourself
    you build a telescope...

You meet your sweetheart, who one day
will be my mother,   and when
you marry   both have stars in your eyes
together   give birth
to a shared dream—
loving family   children four
and a good home
You work hard
to make our dream real
Many happy days we spend
under the sun; many a summer night
★ ★ we camp out ★ ★ ★ ☆
beneath   the stars

Later, you know heartache and pain:
the loss of our beloved house
when your work takes us   halfway
across a continent   and back—
beloved house of your design,
your vision for us;
then   the loss of work
in a time when such
is not expected

But you are like the top
of a tall old pine,
you told me once: tough
like resinous tar—
and you survive
vigorous, unbowed
through your painful silences
and copious speech
as you struggle
to make sense of it all

Gazing through your telescope
you watch the stars
and dream...
In time, you re-discover
timeless child-like joy
in simple things

At 77   you sing to me
of *The Star* ★ — of *Tähti,*
in your Finnish tongue
Voice trembling, eyes moist
you translate that I might
understand:

   Torch of the sparkling infinitude
   Star so pure and unblemished
   Why is thy breast so icy cold?

Your vigour is gone now,
your telescope at rest
Your body after 83 years ails
But though small and frail,
in your old age you are
young   at heart
and your eyes are like *stars*!
radiant
and perfect
your love and peace
illuminate us all

Father, I must tell you this:
I will always see you
in their eyes
whenever I see the stars

...and ever the stars shine on...

BLESS THE CHILD

Child, I once was a child like you
tender   unformed   open to the winds
free to follow the way they blow
free to choose my own chosen road;

Child, oh my child   flesh of my flesh
and bone of my bone, closely I hold you
to my loving breast: yet not so close that
you are not free to draw your own breath,
to know your own need.

Child of earth   of flesh and bone
within you dwells an inborn spirit
of wonder, delight and playful desire
to discover a world; to uncover a dream.

Child, I still am a child: like you
eager to learn,   to follow the winds,
easily loved and easily bruised,
easily torn,   easily soothed;

Child of spirit   closely I hold you
in heart and soul: your gifts to flower
in safety and peace; your dreams to grow,
your trust to form   that one day
you may   with love and affection
and loving protection   bless
with tenderness   a child like you.

SONG TO THE EARTH

Living Breathing Globe   of granite
and vapour,   water and dust;
beloved of trillions from trilobyte to us:
Beneath your teeming tactile crust
beats a heart of fire
fueling firm foundations
on which we live our brief lives,
glimmerings on the vast slate of time.

I, rooted here   in the present
nourished by your bounty
and your loveliness,   grounded
by your wisdom   and your secrets

am awed   by unfathomed
depths of whale-peopled oceans,
palpable silence of huge shifting deserts,
the thunder of a Niagara's fall.

I love to wander
over flowered green hills
of butterfly flutters and bumblebees,
slender vaulted seed spires arched
above grassy fields   where berries
and leaves   weave thicket spells
of bramblewood;   love to ramble
through forested valleys of velvet mists
beside rivers and rills and whippoorwills
and along the shores of great lakes and
periwinkle seas.   I am held captive
on banks of silver streams   mesmerized
by star sparkles and crystal dreams
melodious burblings of clear, cool water
on fluted beds of stone.

Mighty Earth   our mother and lover,
source of sustenance/shelter/hope   within
an immense incomprehensible universe:
    May you endure in eternal beauty
vitality undemolished by dazed humanity's
feverish busy-ness, dizzy growth   excesses
of asphalt and concrete, toxic substances
and other mad pursuits.
    May we learn to love you   with
your own wisdom   and with the passion
of your fire;   with gratitude and respect
commensurate with your gifts;   and with
sweet silver music, like the lyre.
    Magnificent Globe   I humbly aspire
to make of my life   a song, hymn to
your profoundest desire.

Our Lap Luxurious

I come to this place by various ways
yet   it matters not   how
I arrive;   its bountiful
pleasures   are   ever   alive:

I pass by—you draw me down
to your thighs,   wrap
enfolding arms
round this pliant clay.

Perhaps I come   seeking
that   dear   embrace
nestle into my cherished place:
your beloved lap, my love.

Settled within your male
warmth   divine,
arms lapping yours,   entwined
I burrow deep in your fold;

You bury your face
in the curve of my back
clasp me firm in
your comforting hold.

Luxurious   beyond measure,
these riches we treasure
enwrapped   in our lap
of love.

LOVE IS A RIVER

My love is a river
  that flows along your banks, embraces
  your island self,   courses over
      your passionately winding way~
  settles contentedly in still pools.

Your love   like summer rain
  falls on me in warm wet kisses
  streams over me   in sinuous rivers
  floods me with waves of warmth and fire.

Seeing your face in summer rain
  I wash you with kisses of warm love
  rain kisses on your face, your hair
       your neck, your arms
  love you in swelling   oceanic waves.

Your love washes over me   growing,   gathering
  thundering, rushing in nourishing waves of desire
  soothing, smoothing my ruffles in quiet rustles
  of ocean release.

Our love is river,   rain   and ocean
  flowing in rivers and streams of emotion,
  perpetual streams of enduring devotion.   Like rain
    our love   could fill an ocean with rivers
  of constant   fluvial   motion.

ODE TO LOVE

Love, you are the jubilant songbird
    wafted   on a winnowing wind
       the butterfly   fluttering   in a breeze
         the eagle ascending on searing thermals—
            Transport me with wings: let me fly!

Love, oh Love! Radiant ✧ beacon
                ashine with heavenly promise:
Your light—pure bright white—beckons from afar…
Lift my soul up to your heights, your sea-breach!
Broaden my sights to the breadth of your reach!
Shine your starry beams on the ground I tread:
                       Show me the way!

Warm Love! Drawn near, your blessed light
                dazzles   with the lustre of golden sun
   merges past, present, future into one…
Pour your healing warmth on my weary heart
Teach me your gentle and divinest art
Beam your shining rays on my fractious head:
                     Show me your ways!

Love, beautiful Love —
Brilliant many-faceted jewel!
    Each perfect face reflects magnificent you
        moving us to realms   beyond ourselves:
  Unconditional Mother Love is holiest *pearl*
  Father Love — faithful, indomitable — is *diamond*
  Trusting Child Love sweetly shines pure clear *amethyst*
  Familial Love is *garnet*, born of blood and familiarity
  Self-Love—the *tiger's-eye*—underlies a healthy love of all
  Platonic Love is *amber*, respecting another's inner self
  Rosy-eyed, Romantic Love is *ruby*; blind to flaws
  Physical Love, of passionate *sapphire* joins ~ bodies
                    ~ in waves ~ of desire

Topaz—Mate Love cherishes a special, chosen one
Soul-mate Love is **moonstone**—life shared as though
                              two souls were one
Love of Humanity weds merciful *agate* with
                              magical *malachite*
Onyx, Love of Knowledge elevates Λ the mind
Lustrous *opal*, Love of Beauty, lifts the soul   .
Creative Love, of pliant *coral*, builds anew
                              on what has gone before
Love of Life, rare *emerald*, is ever bright; velvet; green
Love of Earth and Nature is timeless; is *jade*
                         is reverence; is healing
Sacred *lapis lazuli* is Spiritual Love—sky-blue   seeing
                         God-Love seeking heavenward
Brilliant   the multiple facets move *us* to reflect   upon you!

Love, you are a deep pool—
Replenisher of souls
          Unending source; mirror; quencher of thirst
     Gazing into your eye
     I am humbled, exalted,
             nearly burst with awe and revelation
     Let me drink from your mouth
     Let me bathe, then immerse
             myself in your holy waters; arise…
     Float lightly in mere skin
     Filled deeply from within.

Oh Love, Bright Star ✰ of heaven's gate,
               Giver and teacher: Steady my soul
          Lead me to my destiny, my long awaited fate
     Strengthen my purpose; guide me to my goal.
     Open, Heart   to Love's gifts of grace:
               Mysteries and visions of a universe ☯ whole.

LOVE GARDEN II

leisurely the narrow path
   winds   through
glossy green fern beds
birch groves papery pink and white
pine woods thick with golden whispers

deep within   hidden
amongst tall trees
lies   a place of dreams:
a secret heart open to the sun

murmuring brooks glint silver;
smooth warm stones edge, encircle
the lotus-blossomed pool   splashed
with touches of blue flag and cattails

silken wind strokes the pines. . .

love,   luscious love
thrills the air with
scents of honeysuckle and rose
and the liquid outpourings of
an impassioned oriole

in wonder   we enter
the secluded garden resplendent
with purple plum, passion flower
and ripe peaches pendant

on a heavy-laden tree
savour firm, moist golden flesh
plump, juicy blackberries
sweet with summer wine

softly, doves coo; softly. . .

TO MY HUSBAND
Nearing Our Silver Anniversary

I remember so clearly, dear...do you?

> *Do you ... take this woman*
> *to be your lawful wedded wife....*
> *And do you ... take this man...?*

our sincere *I do*'s...was it yesterday, then? Yet it
seems we've been   always   together
> *...for better or for worse,*
> *in sickness and in health...*

traced, fingered, felt the beauty of the paired coins:
dwelt in, shared...share a wealth of joy, and the joy
of health; touched, too, the hard edges   weathering
sickness and sorrow with the most we can muster
of patience and dignity,   lending shoulders hands
heart   in time of other's pain or need
  Partners in work   play and life   we've been
in all ways man and wife
> *...to love, honour...*

respect our respective natures, needs and dreams,
sharing a vision of love:

> *We love with tenderness and with reason;*
> *with passion's flame and with the still sea's calm...*

We honour our different-ness: rejoice in
your maleness, my womanliness, each from other
learning ~

~ other ways of doing   and being,
broadening   horizons,   perspectives...

    Friends, lovers, confidants   we share
a vision of life: seek the essentials,   cast away
the superficial; pursue   what we truly love
and what, ultimately, matters; roving meadows,
waters, woods ~ lovers of nature   of her beauty
and her ways, and of our simple life

    In all this we see with each other's eyes, feel
with each other's heart

                 ...'til death do you part?

    Silver clear my answer rings: ***I do!***
Yes, dearest I do ~ with love, with gladness
give my heart to you   but give it not away;
for to you   it but comes home,   to stay.

LOVE MADE WITH LOVE

Love made with love
   shimmers above
      love made with pure heat and motion;
True love expands
   beyond mere glands
      gives rise to deeper emotion.

'Tis love makes love grow
   that lovers may know
      fulfillment of their fullest union;
Hearts truly engaged
   like fine wine when aged
      attain the headiest goal.

With love lovers trace
   through physical grace
      delicious paths to the soul;
True love-making done,
   lovers   blissful as one
      feel the heart of love made whole.

TENDER NIGHTS OF LOVE

With day's work done and the night hours come
our thoughts drift languorously to love...
   Our eyes meet—mine soften as they take you in;
yours lift as you arise.   Flushed, feminine
I follow your lead: we draw together
in tender embrace   withdraw
to our private space . where lights go low;
moving slow   we slip easily into
our rites of love...

   Fondly meander love's sensuous streams
     Under spell of visions revealing
       Surrender to love's irrepressible dreams
        Entrust to the universe of feeling...

It is familiar terrain that we explore, wedded
as we've been for twenty-four years and more.
I know your manscape intimately now: firm
rounded contours of your muscular frame,
fine silvered softness of your deep brown hair,
the revelations of your mysterious grove
just as you know all features of my ground
my every mound and secret cove; still we exult
in exalted realms of touch: savour the silken
smoothness of skin, the voluptuous contact
of our bodies...

   Long attuned to each other's rhythms, we play
     one another like instruments of love, sway
       variations on themes of undulation; in
    finely orchestrated movements you fathom
       my depths as I surround you with
   symphonic vibrations; in concert we hear
     the music of the spheres ~ the mated oneness
       grown profounder, it appears...

Our hallowed rites over, we linger   aglow
blessed anew   through   tender nights of love.

TIGER NIGHTS

then come the tiger nights
when the love in your eyes burns fiercely bright
and our love comes hot in the heat of night
   or beneath a strong sun's blazing light;
when passion floods in tiger fashion
and love pulses fierce in our blood:

    tears tiger bites at flesh's meat
      claws tiger stripes with fiery heat
        snarls tiger urges to fervour's beat

    vaults tiger heights   with surges   of might
and expressed . . . . lies hotly complete.

ORDINARY THINGS

◊ your orderly habits
◊ your exuberant gait
◊ the warm smell of your sun-washed skin
◊ the way you grin at your own waggish humour
◊ your slippers by the door, the ghost of you
in their form and stance
◊ stacks of books strewn about your chair
◊ your cheerfully whistled *Ride of the Valkyries*
◊ our lively discussions on every imaginable thing
◊ our comfortable silences
◊ your eyes tracing shapes within a room
◊ your slow, contemplative pacings
◊ those wornout socks and shoes you hold to like friends
◊ waking to bright-eyed you by my side
◊ your natural, unaffected manner
◊ quick rhythms you lightly tap with chopsticks
◊ your earthy, affectionate nature
◊ the fluent sentences of curiously jumbled thought
you speak so clearly from your sleep
◊ the shared minutiae of our daily lives

my love, dear   thrives   on   ordinary things ◊

ECSTASY

Love's mysteries in souls do grow,
But yet the body is his book...

from *"The Ecstasy,"* by John Donne (1633)

I

Delicate lavender, the lily ~
direct descendant from ancestral
gardens of the Forbidden City
springs   ecstatic   from a
bare patch of fertile ground,
slender spire thrust thigh high
in three fervent days,   resurrected
enthralls us with her ravishing
sculpted beauty.

II

An angled spear of sunlight pierces
woodland air, catches our breath:
reveals   the tiny wide-eyed fawn
motionless   upon   dappled leaf-litter
bed,   concealed   beneath a small
parasol of green ~ curled body circles
the mayapple stem;   unblinking
golden brown gaze   meets ours
    Nearby sounds the watchful doe
    In the distance a proud stag
this diminutive prize their ecstasy.

III

Mutual gifts in love laid bare
join, unite   give birth to miracles
beyond the bounds of island selves.
    You and I   in our intimacy
transcend separateness,   enter
an intuitive realm: pure potentiality,
creative coupling of minds and souls
as potent as our bodies' bliss.
    Through you I touch the universe
together we know the divine ~ move
in streams of unseen air   higher
currents, harmonies and tides where
the mysteries of love   reign   supreme.

REFLECTIONS OF LOVE

Reflections of love are: lovers' faces
by moonlight;   spring peepers trilling
by a still pool; Prokofiev's *Romeo and Juliet,*
and a mother cradling her infant child.

They are   wild roses and bleeding hearts;
sun-kissed daisies   dancing in summer
wind,   and   weeping elephants
mourning   a fallen friend.

They are hand-made quilts and beautifully
crafted homes;   holding hands by daylight;
moonbeams glistening on fresh snow;
and wild animals   free to roam.

Reflections of love are profound respect for
all sentient beings;   and love poems pouring
from my heart; and spontaneous outbursts
in New York proclaiming: *"Frodo Lives!"*

They are laughter and kisses wildly spilled,
and native grasses nodding by a woodland
stream;   pure spring water;   and glassy
willows gleaming on a golden pond.

They are   windsong in white pines;
and fireflies; a thousand small kindnesses;
cherry blossoms in morning mist;   and
sharing the *chi.*

Reflections of love   are mellow thoughts
that percolate past consciousness;   and
you and I in each other's eyes; forgiving
the unforgiveable; and the beauty of
nature, preserved.   *Namaste!*

MEDITATION ON "NAMASTE"

Nam'–as –té :
May love bless your way!
**The good in me honours
the good in thee.**
In my heart you stay,
may love pave your way!
**The peace in me honours
the peace in thee.**
May we thrive on good
and live in peace,
may love bless our way,
Namaste!

QUIET JOY

Such quiet joy, lying wrapped in your arms
Souls anchored close within love's firm embrace.
Breast pressed against breast I caress your face
Nestled secure under sway of love's charms.

Softly rocked by your rising, falling breath
I feel the rhythm of your slow beating heart
Sense our spirits converging, never to part
Not through time nor space, life, nor even death.

In turn I receive you, hold you to stay
Draw you close to my breast, that heart you claim.
You wrap yourself tight round my woman's frame
Enfold me again in your manly way.

This peaceful contentment that we enjoy
Sharing warmth of body, of heart and mind
Draws and secures deep-rooted ties that bind
Here, in lover's arms   rapt with quiet joy.

*Our Love Is A Sacred Thing!**

Like sky-high hawks born to hover   still
upon the breath of the wind;

... like sea-borne feathers floated across time
from shore to distant shore

... like secrets breathed by blazing stars into
dark and hollow traces of paths worn long ago

... like a silver-throated thrush   praising
from hidden places   the forest mysterious

... like altars to the gods in ancient caves
still redolent of ambergris and must

... like newborn lilies lifting pale faces
to worship the rising sun

... like pine-scented sighs and silky whispers
of ages past and of those to come,

Our love is a sacred thing!

---

* This poem was inspired by Armand Silvestre's lovely *"Notre Amour"*

FETED

Mated in this life
Feted husband and wife,
We dwell in our joy!

PRAYER OF THANKS

Gazing upon my garden green
    awash with sun's golden light
    bursting with green grateful life
     buds ripe to burst their blooming beauty!
    alive with rustling, flying, slithering, skittering
    bustling with hops, leaps and bounds . . .
My eyes drink in this God-given beauty
    drink thirstily of green grateful garden
    imbibe luscious meadow and forest beyond;
My ears ring with birdsong
    with voices of wind and of pond...

Gazing, I also burst
    burst into bloom with gladness
    with God-loving gladness
    and grateful *joie de vivre*
     loving the living, loving all the living:
     low and tall, slow and fast, great and small.

Basking in this golden beauty
    full with the God-gift of life,
    I am filled with thankfulness
    with God-loving thankfulness:
     I give thanks, O Lord!
     I give thanks.

TIERCERON PRESS

1998